Petey's Listening Ears

Wisdom For Little Hearts

L.R.Knost

He who has ears, let him hear.

CrossBooks™
A Division of LifeWay
1663 Liberty Drive
Bloomington, IN 47403
www.crossbooks.com
Phone: 1-866-879-0502

First published by CrossBooks: April 12, 2011

ISBN: 978-1-6150-7795-3 (sc)

Printed in the United States of America

This book is printed on acid-free paper.

Illustrations by Derek Knost

Author photograph by Melissa Lynsay Photography

CROSSBOOKS

Dedicated to
Samuel Robert Knost
"Sammy"
June 5, 2009
In my arms for a moment
In my heart forever
Mommy will never forget you, baby boy.

Petey was having a bad day.

First, his daddy said not to pull the cat's tail. But Petey didn't listen. He wanted his bunny friend, Beans, to get a cat-back ride.

The cat scratched Petey's hand!

That made Petey cry.

Then, his mommy said not to dump his toy box out all over the floor. But Petey didn't listen. He wanted to play pirate ship with Beans.

Petey had to spend ALL MORNING picking up his toys!

That made Petey pout.

Then, his sister said not to play with her makeup. But Petey didn't listen. He wanted to play circus clowns with Beans.

Petey had to take a BATH in the middle of the day!

That made Petey mad.

At lunch, Daddy said, "Petey, you're having a bad day, aren't you?" Petey just hung his head and nodded.

Daddy said, "Did you forget to turn on your listening ears today?" Petey's eyes filled with tears, and he nodded again.

Petey's daddy gave him a big hug.

"Why don't you try turning on your listening ears now?" said Daddy. "I bet you'll have a much better day." Petey grinned and twisted the pretend knobs on his ears to turn his listening ears on.

Later, Petey's daddy asked him to turn down the
television. Petey listened, and his daddy gave him
a big thumbs up! That made Petey giggle.

Then, his mommy asked him to come into the kitchen. Petey listened, and his mommy gave him a cookie! That made Petey happy.

Then, his sister told him to put on his coat. Petey listened, and his sister took him to the park to play! That made Petey laugh out loud.

Later, when Daddy tucked Petey into bed and said his
prayers with him, Daddy said, "Turning your listening
ears on was a good idea, wasn't it?" Petey said, "Yes!"
and gave his daddy a great big goodnight hug.

It had turned out to be a good day, after all.

CPSIA information can be obtained at www.ICGtesting.com
225363LV00002B